Date Due

MATTHEW HENSON

CO-DISCOVERER OF THE NORTH POLE

Julian May

Illustrated by PHERO THOMAS

CREATIVE EDUCATIONAL SOCIETY, Inc.
Mankato, Minnesota 56001

ISBN: 87191-218-X
Library of Congress Catalog Card Number: 72-85038

MATTHEW HENSON

CO-DISCOVERER OF THE NORTH POLE

A young black boy walked along the Baltimore waterfront. Tall sailing ships lay at anchor there in that year of 1879. Soon they would sail to far parts of the world, and the boy wanted to go with them.

He walked boldly up to an old man who wore a captain's uniform. "Please, sir. Are you the captain of this ship?"

"That I am," the old man said. "Captain Childs, master of the steam merchantman *Katie Hines*."

"I need a job," the boy said. "I walked all the way from Washington, D.C. to become a sailor. Take me, Captain! I'll work hard."

"You will, will you?" The captain smiled. "What's your name?"

"Matthew Alexander Henson," said the boy. "I'm twelve years old. *You* can call me Matt."

The captain was a kindly man. He asked young Matt many questions and learned that his parents were dead. An idea came to the old sailor. In those days, many people thought that blacks could not learn. Black children did not often go to school. But Captain Childs believed that skin color had nothing to do with brain power.

He could tell that Matt was a smart lad. So he hired him as cabin boy. Before the ship sailed, Captain Childs bought a pile of school books. He was going to use young Matt to prove that black children could learn.

The steam sailing ship *Katie Hines* went to Hong Kong. And every day of the voyage was a schoolday for Matt. He learned seamanship from the crew, but he also studied each day in the captain's cabin. Captain Childs taught him to read and write and do arithmetic.

After a year, Matt was promoted from cabin boy to able seaman. The ship went to Europe, North Africa and Russia as well as to ports in Asia. Matt studied geography, history, astronomy and navigation. He became an excellent carpenter and mechanic.

For five years, he followed the sea. Then Captain Childs, who had treated him like a father, died. Broken-hearted, Matt tried sailing on another ship. But not all captains were as full of good will toward blacks as Captain Childs had been. Matt discovered prejudice and hatred.

Discouraged, he took jobs on land. But nothing made him happy. He was 21 years old in 1887 when he met the man who would change his life.

Matt was working as a stock clerk in a Washington hat store. His intelligence had impressed the owner.

One day a young naval officer came in. "I am going to the rain forest of Nicaragua," he said. "A sun helmet is about the last thing I will need—besides a good man-servant. But not many servants would dare travel to such a wild place."

The hat store owner said, "I know a young man who may be eager for adventure." And he called Matt.

The officer and the black man stared at each other. Matt saw a very tall man, ten years older than himself, with a sweeping moustache. His blue eyes were stern. He had an air of great self-confidence. The officer's name was Lieutenant Robert E. Peary.

A strange feeling came over Matt as the officer talked about the job he was offering. To be a servant . . . that hurt Matt's pride. But it was a chance to escape from the dull life he had followed since giving up the sea.

Matt took a deep breath. "I'd like the job, sir."

Two weeks later, he was on his way to Central America.

Matt worked as a servant for only three months. Then Peary promoted him to a job he liked much better—working on the survey crew. Matt helped lay out a route for a canal that had been proposed for Nicaragua. It was dangerous, uncomfortable work but always exciting.

Six months later, when the canal survey was done, Peary said to Matt: "My real interests do not lie in the tropics but rather in the Far North. Last year I began to explore Greenland. I am determined to be the first man to cross that big island's icecap. You're a good man, Matt. Would you like to come with me?"

Matt agreed. But it was three years before Peary could raise money for an expedition. And he was not the first to cross Greenland. That feat was accomplished by a Norwegian, Fridtjof Nansen. Peary decided to explore northern Greenland instead.

In June, 1891, the Peary North Greenland Expedition set sail. Matt was aboard as manservant and handyman. There were two scientists, John Verhoeff and Langdon Gibson, who planned to study Greenland's geology, weather, birds and animals. There was a young doctor, Frederick Cook, who in later years would also become an arctic explorer. There was a Norwegian ski champion, Eivind Astrup, who would help Peary explore the icecap.

And there was Peary's beautiful young bride, Josephine!

As the ship sailed northward, Matt was hard at work building prefabricated sections of the house that they would live in. He wondered what Greenland would be like.

Before the ship sailed, some of Matt's friends told him he was a fool to go. "Your ancestors came from Africa, a hot land. You won't last long in a place full of ice and snow. The temperature gets down to 60 below! Winter is eight months long, and part of that time, the sun doesn't even come up!"

They told Matt about two United States arctic expeditions that had ended in disaster. Lt. George DeLong of the U.S. Navy tried to sail into the Arctic Ocean west of Alaska. His ship was crushed in the ice. He and 11 men died trying to walk over the frozen ocean to Siberia, while 24 men survived.

And in 1881 the U.S. Army sent Major Adolphus Greely to Ellesmere Land, an island next to Greenland. Two supply ships were unable to reach the expedition. Of its 24 men, 17 starved to death.

The hardships of the Peary Expedition began even as they sailed. During a storm at sea, Peary's leg was broken. But he refused to turn back. They sailed into McCormick Bay on the West Greenland coast. While Matt set up their shelter, Red Cliff House, Peary sent the other men to find Eskimos.

These people of the Northland were brown-skinned and narrow-eyed, members of the Mongoloid race. They knew how to survive in this terrible land. Peary was convinced that the only way arctic exploration could succeed was with Eskimo help.

Several Eskimo families agreed to work for Peary. They would help with the hunting, provide dogs and dogsleds, and the Eskimo women would make warm fur clothes for the explorers.

When the Eskimos first saw Matt's brown face, they became very excited.

"Innuit! Innuit!" they cried happily.

The word meant "soul" or "person." It was the Eskimos' name for themselves. They had decided that Matt was really an Eskimo brother from the Land of the South. Matt was very friendly to the Eskimos and they learned to love him. Their name for him was *Miy paluk,* "dear Mattie."

All through the winter, the Eskimos taught Matt their language. He learned how to hunt caribou, seal and walrus. And most important, Matt became an expert driver of the snarling, half-wild native dogs.

In spring, 1892, the expedition laid out supply dumps along the route Peary planned to explore. Then Peary and Astrup alone set out on the trip across the top of Greenland. It was May 24 when they left.

All through June and into July, Matt and the others went about their business at Red Cliff House. It was warm, and the snow melted along the coast. Flowers bloomed. But only a few miles inland the icecap rose up thousands of feet—an eternal wilderness of snow and ice, without plants or animals.

In late July, the ship returned to take them home. But there was still no sign of the two explorers. It was not until August 6 that Peary and Astrup staggered into camp —thin, sore and partly snowblind. Most of their dogs had died, but they had walked 1,200 miles to the east coast of Greenland and back.

It was a triumph! But then tragedy struck, shortly before they left. Verhoeff, the geologist, went off alone and did not return. Matt led a search party. But all they found was a deep hole where Verhoeff had broken through a thin crust of snow and plunged to an icy death in a deep crevasse.

Much as he regretted Verhoeff's death, Peary could think of little besides his plans for a new expedition. Back in the United States, Peary took Matt with him on a money-raising tour. This time they would march northward—to the Pole itself!

The tour was a great success. Peary set up a model Eskimo village on stage and lectured in a fur outfit. At a signal, Matt would come on stage, driving a small team of Eskimo dogs.

By June, 1893, Peary was ready to go north again. This time he had the best equipment—but he had not selected his people so well.

Disaster lay ahead.

Mrs. Peary was with them again. She brought a nurse, since she was expecting a baby. Astrup and Matt were old arctic hands. But the other nine members of the expedition were college-educated "gentlemen" that Peary had selected merely because he liked them.

After building a new house, the expedition tried to lay supply dumps. But the college men were inexperienced and even foolhardy. Matt had to rescue some of them from disaster. Many of the others were crippled by injuries.

In spring, when the "push for the Pole" began, the party was able to travel only 124 miles. Poor management, very bad weather and injuries caused the failure.

The ship came in August, but Peary did not want to go home. A proud man, he could not stand defeat.

"Some of us might stay and make another try next year," he said. "Who's with me?"

"I am, sir," said Matt.

"And I," said a young newspaperman, Hugh Johnson Lee. But all the others refused to remain, thinking that Peary was mad. Mrs. Peary would have stayed, but her husband sent her and the baby home. She promised to raise money for the expedition.

In the spring of 1895, Peary, Matt and Lee sledged across Greenland and arrived at the spot that Peary and Astrup had reached in 1892. But they had used up all their food. Only 11 of their 42 dogs were still alive, and Lee's feet were frozen so he could not walk.

"We'll never reach the Pole," Peary groaned as they made camp. "We'll be lucky to get back alive."

A herd of musk-oxen saved them. Peary and Matt hunted them for meat. An enraged cow almost trampled Peary, but Matt managed to kill the animal with his last bullet.

Then came the terrible return journey. Lee had to ride all the way. The musk-ox meat gave out when they were still 200 miles from home, so they had to eat the dogs, one by one. When only a single dog was left, Matt and Peary joined it in pulling Lee on the sled.

Then they ate the last of the food. Stumbling, falling, crawling along, they traveled for three more days before they finally reached the expedition camp—one black man, two white men, and a scrawny Eskimo dog.

Mrs. Peary came with a ship in August to take them home. She had raised money for the trip only with great difficulty. But Peary had an idea.

They sailed down the Greenland coast to Cape York. There lay three large meteorites which the Eskimos called the Dog, the Woman, and the Tent. If Peary could bring them back, they could be sold to a museum.

Matt and the Eskimos managed to load the Dog and Woman on board. But the Tent, a huge piece of nickel-iron weighing 34 tons, was too heavy.

Back in New York, Peary sold the meteorites to the American Museum of Natural History. And Matt found work there as a taxidermist, preparing exhibits of arctic animals—many of which he had collected himself.

During the next three years, Matt worked happily at the museum. He took time off for two short expeditions with Peary, attempts to secure the last big meteorite. The 1896 attempt failed, but in 1897 they succeeded. The Tent, now called the Ahnighito Meteorite, was brought to the museum. Peary was rewarded—not only with money, but with honors and the backing of powerful men.

He was able to set out on a new expedition in 1898. He chose Matt as his assistant, even though some people objected to the idea of a black man as an explorer.

But Peary said, "I need Matt Henson. No other man knows the Eskimos or the Northland so well."

Peary's new plan was to set up a base much further north—at Fort Conger on Ellesmere Island, the abandoned camp of the tragic Greely Expedition. From there they would explore the northernmost part of Greenland to see if land extended all the way to the Pole.

The base was established. But in doing so, Peary froze his feet badly and lost his toes. Matt and the Eskimo assistants brought him back to Greenland, where he took a year to recover.

In spring and summer of 1900, Peary, Matt, and six Eskimos explored the north coast of Greenland.

The land stopped 450 miles south of the Pole. To attain their goal, they would have to cross the pack ice of the Arctic Ocean.

Returning to Fort Conger, they spent a long winter. In April, 1901, they marched directly north. But Peary's strength gave out. They had to turn back before they even reached the ocean.

During these explorations, Matt never questioned Peary's judgment. Often the Eskimos refused to go on. They believed that devils lived out on the pack ice, as well as on the Greenland icecap. But Matt, speaking their tongue far better than Peary, was able to persuade most of them to go on.

When Peary was sick, Matt nursed him. When they needed food, Matt hunted. But strangely enough, the two men were not what we would call friends. Peary was never able to call a black man friend. He respected Matt—even loved him—but still kept the prejudices that were deeply rooted in him.

In 1902 they tried again for the Pole. Peary, Matt, and the Eskimos Sipsoo, Angmalokto, Ootah and Pooblah went out onto the mountainous piles of sea ice. It was 45 below zero. The ice groaned and cracked beneath their feet.

Each mile that they traveled seemed like five, so difficult was the going. Finally they reached a wide area of open water, called a lead. They waited, but it would not freeze. With the Pole still 343 nautical miles away, they turned back.

"The game is off," Peary wrote in his diary. "My dream of 16 years is ended."

In despair, Peary and Matt returned to the United States. It was necessary for Matt to find a job, so he became a Pullman porter on the railroads. He enjoyed traveling all over the country—especially since he could ride instead of walk!

Two years went by while Peary worked hard to raise money for another try at the Pole. It was a matter of American honor, he told people. "We must nail the Stars and Stripes to the North Pole!"

Matt met a beautiful girl named Lucy Ross and fell in love. But then Peary wrote to him asking him to go on another expedition.

Matt told Lucy, "We must wait until I return. I'll bring you the North Pole for a wedding present."

But this trip was also destined for failure. In the spring of 1906, Peary, Matt and Ootah reached a place on the sea ice 174 miles from the Pole. It was a new record for farthest north.

But they were running out of food. Support parties, which were supposed to keep them supplied, were cut off by leads of open water.

"We've got to turn back, Matt," Peary said. "We're licked once again."

Later, in the ship returning home, Peary's old ambitions revived. "We'll come back," he told Matt. "We'll come back next year and win the Pole yet."

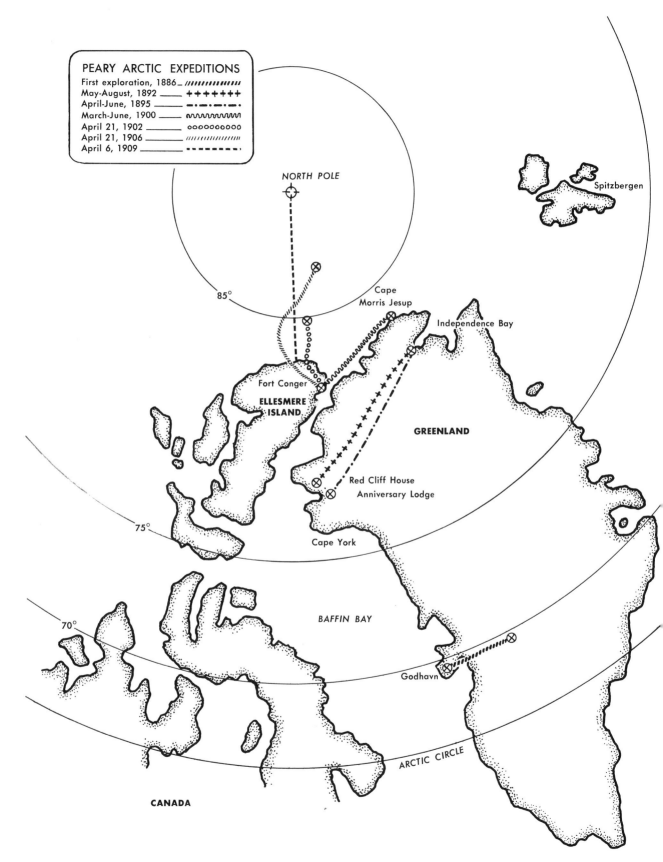

PEARY ARCTIC EXPEDITIONS
First exploration, 1886 _ ///////////////
May-August, 1892 _____ +++++++
April-June, 1895 _____ —·—·—·—·
March-June, 1900 _____ ∿∿∿∿∿∿∿
April 21, 1902 _____ ooooooooo
April 21, 1906 _____ ///////////////
April 6, 1909 _____ — — — — —

NORTH POLE

Spitzbergen

85°

Cape
Morris Jesup

Independence Bay

Fort Conger

ELLESMERE
ISLAND

GREENLAND

75°

Red Cliff House
Anniversary Lodge

Cape York

70°

BAFFIN BAY

Godhavn

ARCTIC CIRCLE

CANADA

Their ship, the *Roosevelt,* had been badly damaged by the ice. Peary asked Matt to stay with the vessel in New York and supervise repairs.

The American public and press were becoming tired of Peary's failures. Although brave, he had a raspy manner that did not win friends. He was now 50 years old, a limping cripple. He had flown in the face of tradition by having a black man as his chief assistant.

Nonetheless, Peary was determined to make one final try at the Pole. The ship was repaired and funds were finally gathered together.

Meanwhile, Matt married Lucy Ross in 1907 and had a few months of happiness before embarking on his last arctic expedition.

On July 8, 1908, the ship was ready to sail. President Teddy Roosevelt came on board and declared: "Peary, if any man can reach the Pole, that man will be you!"

Once they had set up their North Ellesmere base, Peary called his men together.

"All of you have important work to do, setting up supply dumps on the way to the Pole. But Henson is the man who will go all the way."

The others had to agree. They were Captain Bob Bartlett of the *Roosevelt;* Professor Ross Marvin, who had been on the last expedition; Dr. Goodsell, the ship's doctor; and two young athletes named George Borup and Donald MacMillan. None could match Matt's 18 years of experience in the North. They agreed that the honor of accompanying Peary to the Pole belonged to Matt Henson.

With 19 Eskimos and 150 dogs, the party set out for the Pole on February 28, 1909. After a fine beginning, they were stopped by a huge lead—perhaps the same one that had cut them off in previous years. After six days, a thin skin of ice formed and they were able to march on.

Many Eskimos were fearful and wanted to turn back, despite the rewards Peary had promised them. Even Ootah was afraid. Peary urged Matt to talk to them. Finally Ootah said:

"If *Miy paluk* goes, I will go, too." And the other Eskimos agreed as well.

As they moved northward, one support party after another dumped supplies, then turned back. Their work was done.

Captain Bartlett was the last to leave Peary and Matt on April 1.

Saying good-bye to Matt, Bartlett whispered, "Commander Peary is dead tired. Most of this final push is going to depend on you."

Matt smiled. "Don't worry. We'll make it." The two men shook hands and then Bartlett was gone.

Four Eskimos—Ootah, Seegloo, Egingwah, and Ookeah—stayed with Peary and Matt. They had four sledges loaded with food and a fifth for a spare. Their 40 dogs were strong, and there seemed no reason why they should not reach the Pole, which was now 132 miles away, within five or six days.

Peary weakened rapidly and Matt had to insist that he ride for part of the way. Once Matt fell through the ice. But Ootah grabbed him by the collar and hauled him out, then helped him into dry clothes.

They pressed on, over pack ice that was not too rough. Within reach of his goal, Peary was so excited that he could not sleep. He was in great pain but also full of joy. On April 5, he took out his sextant and "shot the sun" to determine how far north they were.

"I make our position as 35 miles from the Pole, Matt! Tomorrow's march should bring us there."

At ten in the morning on April 6, Peary called a halt. "We will camp here," he said. Then taking out his sextant, he made a calculation. "I make it 89 degrees, 57 minutes north. We are within three miles of the Pole. At last! At last!"

They built igloos, ate and rested. Peary took photographs, including a famous one of Matt and the Eskimos, each holding a flag. Ookeah held the Navy League banner. Ootah had Peary's fraternity flag. Egingwah held the peace flag of the Daughters of the American Revolution. Seegloo had the Red Cross flag.

But Matthew Henson held the Stars and Stripes.

They sledged back and forth over an area of eight to ten miles in all directions, to be sure that they passed over the Pole. Their instruments, they knew, were not perfectly accurate. But Peary was as certain as a man could be in the early Twentieth Century that he had indeed reached the North Pole.

They stayed only a day, then began the long journey back. The Eskimos were amazed and said to Matt: "What is so special about this spot, Miy? It looks no different from any other place on the ice. How can this be the goal Pearyaksoah has searched for so long?"

Matt tried to explain that the North Pole was invisible. But the Eskimos could not understand. The journey back was made swiftly—and a good thing, for Peary was ill. He had collapsed after winning his great victory.

As they reached solid land, Ootah said, "The Devil of the North is having trouble with his wife, or we would not have returned so easily."

The expedition packed up and sailed southward. Peary had heard strange rumors. Dr. Frederick Cook, who had been on Peary's first real expedition in Greenland, was supposed to have been in the Arctic. He had even said he would try to reach the North Pole!

Stopping at a Greenland village, they happened to meet the two Eskimos who had accompanied Cook.

"We marched with him onto the Frozen Sea," the Eskimos told Matt. "But never were we out of sight of land."

Nonetheless, when Peary and his party reached New York, they received a dreadful surprise. Dr. Cook claimed to have reached the Pole nearly a year before the Peary Expedition.

And what was more, most of the world seemed to believe him!

It was a dismal end to their triumph. Boos greeted the *Roosevelt* as it sailed through the Hudson River in New York. Peary hid himself away to recover from his illness and the unexpected blow to his pride. He left Matt to do as he pleased, so Matt got a job as handyman in a garage.

Then a promoter came to Matt and convinced him to go on a lecture tour, telling the "truth" about the Peary Expedition. The tour was not a success. People had made up their minds that likable Dr. Cook—not grumpy Commander Peary—was telling the truth.

But as months went by, the real story began to emerge. Dr. Cook refused to submit scientific observations that would confirm his trip to the pole. Then he submitted some papers which a committee of scientists said were worthless.

Peary's observations, on the other hand, proved to be genuine. The explorer began to appear in public again. He was given medals and other honors. Cook went to live in South America and Peary was proclaimed the first man to reach the North Pole.

Matt, meanwhile, still worked at his garage job. He wrote a book, *A Negro Explorer at the North Pole,* and lived quietly with his wife, Lucy.

He never saw Peary again. Proud and prejudiced to the last, the explorer saw nothing wrong in cutting himself off from the black man who had been his faithful assistant for nearly 22 years. In 1920, Peary died.

Matt's honors came first from black organizations. Later, as race prejudice began to die in the United States, he was rewarded in other ways. In 1937 he was elected to membership in the famous Explorer's Club—and so was Ootah, the only Eskimo of the polar party still living. In 1945 the Congress of the United States gave Matt a silver medal.

In 1954, 45 years after he had reached the Pole, Matt was honored personally by President Eisenhower. He died a year later, at the age of 88.

His home state of Maryland honored him with a plaque in the State House. It reads:

MATTHEW ALEXANDER HENSON
CO-DISCOVERER OF THE NORTH POLE WITH
ADMIRAL ROBERT EDWIN PEARY
APRIL 6, 1909
BORN: AUGUST 8, 1866   DIED: MARCH 9, 1955

SON OF MARYLAND
EXEMPLIFICATION OF COURAGE, FORTITUDE AND PATRIOTISM,
WHOSE VALIANT DEEDS OF NOBLE DEVOTION
UNDER THE COMMAND OF ADMIRAL ROBERT EDWIN PEARY,
IN PIONEER ARCTIC EXPLORATION AND DISCOVERY,
ESTABLISHED EVERLASTING PRESTIGE AND GLORY
FOR HIS STATE AND COUNTRY